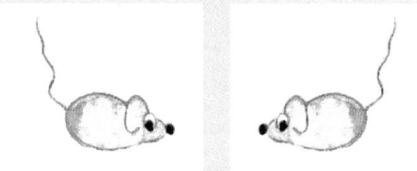

For Carter, Genevieve,
and children everywhere
who enjoy reading.

Copyright © 2016
Freda M. Chaney
All Rights Reserved
Printed in the USA

First Edition
July 7, 2016
Full Color

Story and book design by Freda M. Chaney
Book cover and interior illustrations by Vicki L. Lowery

ISBN-13: 978-1523783670
ISBN-10: 1523783672

Kate Won't Wait!

My sister, Kate, WON'T wait!

Because she's Mama's

FAVORITE

she gets her way

right now!

But I wait

HALF A CENTURY

for Mom to show me how!

But Kate WON'T wait!

She's tardy in the morning!

She questions noon and night!

Mama meets

her EVERY need,

and so we fuss

and fight!

Why don't you hear me, Mama?

You ALWAYS hear dear Kate!

Since she was born,

I feel left out.

All I do is

wait

wait

wait!

But Kate WON'T wait!

Aaaahhhhhhhh!

She's tardy in the morning!

She questions

noon

and night!

Is it OK to be short?
Or tall?

How long does it take to grow up?

Why am I a girl and not a boy?

Mama meets her

EVERY need,

and so we fuss and fight!

If Dr. Ross could take her back,

I'd give him ALL

my money!

I'd throw in my LEGO®

and Boy Scout pack

if he'd only take my

sister back!

But

funny…

I think that I

might miss her.

I think that I CAN wait.

I would miss the

fussing with her

and teasing sister Kate.

She's tardy in the morning.

She questions noon

and night!

When?

How?

Who?

Mama meets her EVERY need,

and so we fuss and fight!

And that's all right!

"Mama, may I have a puppy?"

"Sure, dear Henry!"

The End

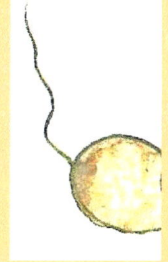

A Keen Mother-Daughter Team

Left to right: Freda M. Chaney, author
Vicki L. Lowery, illustrator

About the Author

Freda M. Chaney has a background in preschool teaching with a doctorate in divinity. She has worked as a youth advocate and in book sales for Scholastic Books. In addition, Freda has published numerous books of her own. Her work has been critiqued in *Writer's Digest*, and published in *Guideposts for Kids*, *Angels on Earth*, *Lyric*, *Midwest Poetry Review*, and many others.

Kate Won't Wait was originally a poem from a collection created by Freda as part of a requirement for the Elementary Education Children's Literature course at Otterbein College. The original title was *Kate Can't Wait!*

• • •

About the Illustrator

Vicki L. Lowery has taught preschool, owned her own business, created numerous murals and posters, and collectable art in watercolors and acrylics. She is the mother of two precocious children who give her plenty of inspiration for her art.

Vicki and Freda travel together to promote and launch books. In 2015, they attended the Writers in Warwickshire festival in England where authors and artists gathered to present their best creative projects at the restored Astley Castle.

Find **Kate Won't Wait**
on Amazon, or
at your local library
and independent bookstores.

...

Freda and Vicki are available
for readings and book signings.
Contact them at chaney@ecr.net.

...

For classroom study and
reading enhancement:
Kate Won't Wait
Teacher's Edition

Made in United States
Orlando, FL
16 October 2024